Contents

Some words are shown in bold, **like this**. You can find out what they mean by looking in the Glossary.

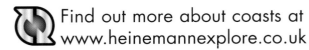
Find out more about coasts at
www.heinemannexplore.co.uk

What is a coast?

A coast is land that lies next to the sea. The sea covers most of the Earth. The **seashore** and **beach** are where the sea splashes against the land.

My World of Geography

COASTS

Angela Royston

Schools Library and Information Services

young Explorer

www.heinemann.co.uk/library
Visit our website to find out more information about **Heinemann Library** books.

To order:
☎ Phone 44 (0) 1865 888066
▤ Send a fax to 44 (0) 1865 314091
▣ Visit the Heinemann Bookshop at www.heinemann.co.uk/library to browse our catalogue and order online.

First published in Great Britain by Heinemann Library, Halley Court, Jordan Hill, Oxford OX2 8EJ, part of Harcourt Education.
Heinemann is a registered trademark of Harcourt Education Ltd.

Editorial: Andrew Farrow and Dan Nunn
Design: Ron Kamen and Celia Jones
Illustrations: Jo Brooker (p.17), Jeff Edwards (p. 5), Art Construction and Darrell Warner (pp. 28–29)
Picture Research: Rebecca Sodergren, Melissa Allison and Debra Weatherley
Production: Duncan Gilbert

Originated by Ambassador Litho Ltd
Printed and bound in China by South China Printing Co Ltd

The paper used to print this book comes from sustainable resources.

ISBN 0 431 11802 7 (hardback)
08 07 06 05 04
10 9 8 7 6 5 4 3 2 1

ISBN 0 431 11807 8 (paperback)
09 08 07 06 05
10 9 8 7 6 5 4 3 2 1

British Library Cataloguing in Publication Data

Royston, Angela
    Coasts. – (My world of geography)
    1. Coasts – Juvenile literature
    I. Title
    551.4'57

A full catalogue record for this book is available from the British Library.

Acknowledgements

The Publishers would like to thank the following for permission to reproduce photographs:

Corbis pp. **4**, **8**, **9** (Brandon D. Cole), **10** (David Muench), **11** (Kevin Morris), **14** (Neil Rabinowitz), **16** (Bill Ross), **19** (Yan Arthus-Bertrand), **21** (Macduff Everton), **22**, **23** (Tony Arruza); Ecoscene pp. **20** (Quentin Bates), **27** (Erik Schaffer); Geoscience Features p. **18** (Dr B. Booth); Getty Images/Photodisc pp. **6**, **12**, **25**; Panos Pictures p. **24** (Guy Mansfield); Photo Library Wales p. **15** (Dave Newbould); Science Photo Library pp. **7** (Jon Wilson), **13** (Jon Wilson); Still Pictures p. **26** (Ray Pfortner).

Cover photograph reproduced with permission of Corbis.

Every effort has been made to contact copyright holders of any material reproduced in this book. Any omissions will be rectified in subsequent printings if notice is given to the Publishers.

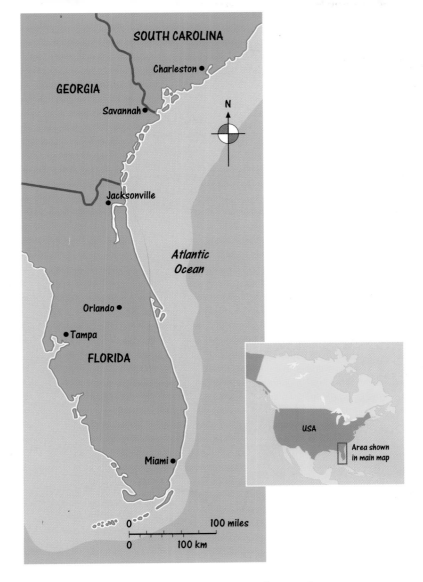

This map shows a stretch of coast.
On a map the sea is usually coloured
blue. Deep water is a darker blue.
The land is coloured green or brown.

Beaches

Some **beaches** are covered with sand. The wind blows the sand into hills called **dunes**. Other beaches are covered with mud. Worms and **shellfish** live on sandy and muddy beaches.

sand dunes

sand

Some beaches are covered with **pebbles** or shells. Not many animals live on pebbly beaches.

Rocks

Many parts of the coast have no **beach**. The **seashore** is just bare rock. Sometimes steep **cliffs** separate the land from the sea.

rock

cliff

Many kinds of animals live on rocky **seashores**. Some live in **rock pools**. Others cling to the rocks. Different kinds of **seaweeds** cling to the rocks too.

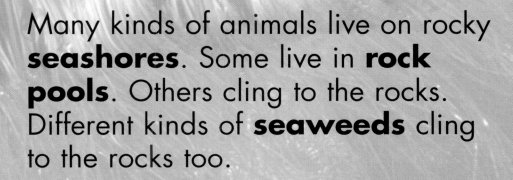

seaweed

starfish

Starfishes, sea anemones and seaweed live in this rock pool.

sea anemone

Salty swamps

A **swamp** is an area of wet, soggy land. In some places on the coast, the sea **floods** part of the land. This turns the land into a salty swamp.

Most plants cannot grow in salty water. But in hot places mangrove trees grow well in salty swamps. **Roots** grow down from the trees' branches into the swamp.

roots

11

Waves

Waves hit the **seashore** all the time. When the sea is stormy, the waves are bigger and more powerful.

12

Waves slowly wear away the rocks and **cliffs**. The rocks crack and crumble to form large stones, **pebbles** and sand.

pebbles

As *the waves crash on to the seashore, the pebbles rub against each other and become round and smooth.*

Caves and bays

Some rocks are hard. Other rocks are soft. The sea wears away soft rocks faster than hard rocks. A **cave** forms when waves wear away a patch of soft rock in a **cliff**.

cave

A **bay** forms where the sea wears away a long stretch of soft rock. The hard rock on each side wears away much more slowly. It sticks out into the sea and forms a **headland**.

headlands

bays

Ragged coasts

A coast shapes the edge of the land. A ragged coast includes many **headlands** and **bays**. A headland sticks out into the sea. A bay lets the sea go further inland.

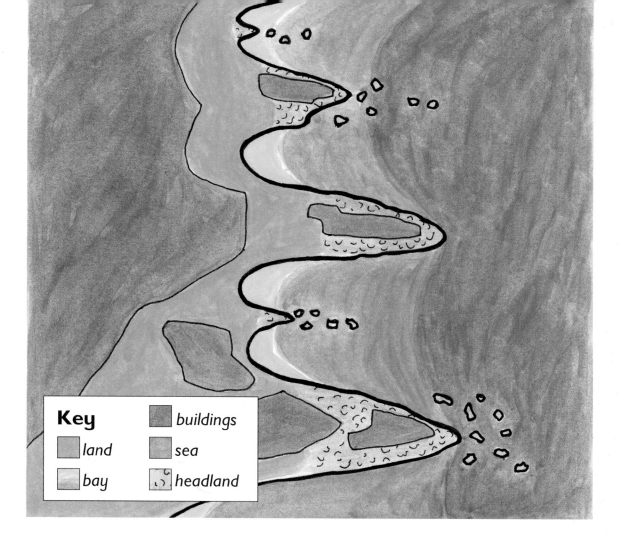

Key
land
bay
buildings
sea
headland

This map shows the same bit of coast as the photo on page 16. You can see the shape of the coast made by the headlands and the bays. You can draw a map like this.

Forming new land

Sometimes the sea sweeps sand and **pebbles** from one part of the coast to another. As the sand and pebbles pile up, new land forms.

This lighthouse used to be at the edge of the sea.

spit

Rivers help to build new land at the **seashore**. Rivers carry soil and stones into the sea. If the sea is shallow, the soil and stones pile up to form a **spit**.

Food from the seashore

Many **shellfish** live on the **seashore**. People catch shellfish to eat as food. They gather mussels, crabs and lobsters by hand.

This special basket for catching lobsters is called a lobster pot.

20

Many kinds of fish live in the sea close to the seashore. People catch fish with rods or nets. This boy has caught shrimps in his net.

Ports and harbours

Some towns and cities are built along the **seashore**. A port is a town or city where ships can load and unload **goods**. People build **docks** where ships can tie up.

Cranes load and unload goods from big ships.

harbour

pier

A **harbour** is part of the seashore that is sheltered from the wind and waves. Sometimes people build a **pier** to make the water in the harbour even more sheltered.

Enjoying the seashore

Many towns on the coast are **holiday resorts**. People go to these resorts to enjoy the **seashore**. Some resorts have sandy **beaches** where people like to swim.

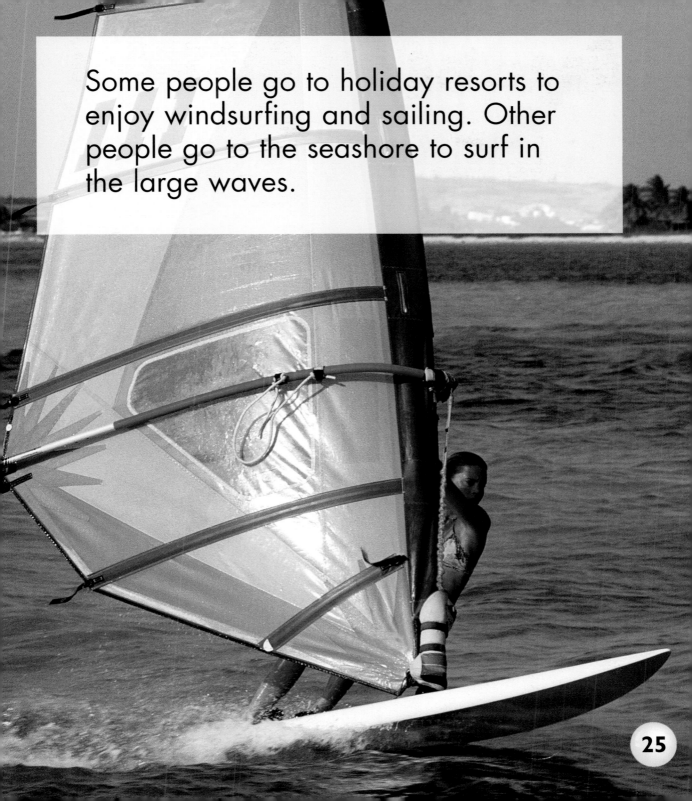

Some people go to holiday resorts to enjoy windsurfing and sailing. Other people go to the seashore to surf in the large waves.

Coasts in danger

People are damaging the **seashore**. In some places, waste from homes and factories flows into the sea. The waste **pollutes** the sea and is washed on to the **beach**.

The sea is wearing away some parts of the seashore. The people who lived in the houses on the edge of this **cliff** had to leave their homes.

Coasts fact file

cliffs

sand dune

pebbles

seaweed

rocks

Find out more about coasts at
www.heinemannexplore.co.uk

This picture shows some of the different things you might find on a **seashore**. The level of the sea changes during the day. This is called the tide. The highest level is the high tide. The lowest level is the low tide.

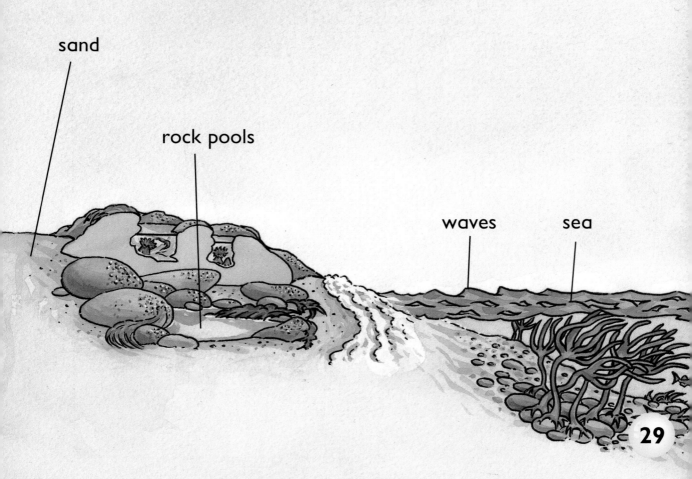

sand

rock pools

waves

sea

Glossary

bay part of the coastline where the sea flows further inland

beach stretch of seashore covered by sand, mud, pebbles or shells

cave large hole or hollow

cliff a steep slope of rock

docks concrete platforms built in a harbour where ships can unload

dune hill made of sand

flood when water from the sea or a river covers the land

goods things that are made, bought and sold

harbour sheltered part of the sea at the coast where boats can tie up

headland piece of land that sticks into the sea

holiday resort town or city where people go on holiday

pebble a round, smooth stone on the seashore

pier a large platform or wall built into the sea

pollute make something dirty

rock pool a pool of salty water among the rocks on a beach

root part of a plant that takes in water from the soil

seashore flat strip of land between the sea and the countryside

seaweed plants that grow in the sea

shellfish animals that have a shell and live in water

spit strip of new land that forms at some places on the coast

swamp wet, soggy ground

Find out more

Further reading

Geography First: Coastlines by Kay Barnham (Hodder Wayland, 2004)

Go Facts: Coral Reefs by Paul McEvoy and Katy Pike (A & C Black, 2003)

Question Time: Seashore by Angela Wilkes (Kingfisher, 2001)

Geography Starts Here: Maps and Symbols by Angela Royston (Hodder Wayland, 2001)

Useful Websites

http://mbgnet.mobot.org/salt/sandy/ – information about different kinds of beaches – muddy, sandy and rocky.

www.teacherxpress.com/f.php?gid=25&id=4 – information from the BBC about coasts and how they are changing, particularly in the UK.

www.cadburylearningzone.co.uk/environment/gallery/ galleryframe.htm – click on the second (purple) Yowie to get information about rocky shores and the Great Barrier Reef off Australia.

Disclaimer

All the Internet addresses (URLs) given in this book were valid at the time of going to press. However, due to the dynamic nature of the Internet, some addresses may have changed, or sites may have changed or ceased to exist since publication. While the author and the Publishers regret any inconvenience this may cause readers, no responsibility for any such changes can be accepted by either the author or the Publishers.

Index